20 FUN FACTS ABOUT BALD EAGLES

BY SHANNON H. HARTS

 Gareth Stevens
PUBLISHING

Please visit our website, www.garethstevens.com. For a free color catalog of all our high-quality books, call toll free 1-800-542-2595 or fax 1-877-542-2596.

Library of Congress Cataloging-in-Publication Data

Names: Harts, Shannon H, author.
Title: 20 fun facts about bald eagles / Shannon H Harts.
Description: New York : Gareth Stevens Publishing, [2021] | Series: Fun
   fact file: North American animals | Includes index.
Identifiers: LCCN 2019045199 | ISBN 9781538257456 (library binding) | ISBN
   9781538257432 (paperback) | ISBN 9781538257449 (6 Pack) | ISBN 9781538257463
   (ebook)
Subjects: LCSH: Bald eagle–Juvenile literature.
Classification: LCC QL696.F32 H374 2021 | DDC 598.9/43–dc23
LC record available at https://lccn.loc.gov/2019045199

First Edition

Published in 2021 by
Gareth Stevens Publishing
111 East 14th Street, Suite 349
New York, NY 10003

Designer: Sarah Liddell
Editor: Kate Mikoley

Photo credits: Cover, p. 1 (main) FloridaStock/Shutterstock.com; file folder used throughout David Smart/Shutterstock.com; binder clip used throughout luckyraccoon/Shutterstock.com; wood grain background used throughout ARENA Creative/Shutterstock.com; p. 5 cvrestan/Shutterstock.com; p. 6 Tom Clausen/Shutterstock.com; p. 8 Rocky Grimes/Shutterstock.com; p. 9 CK_Images/Shutterstock.com; p. 10 Frank Fichtmueller/Shutterstock.com; p. 11 Tracy Kerestesh/Shutterstock.com; p. 12 Martin Rudlof Photography/Shutterstock.com; p. 13 Michael Meshcheryakov/Shutterstock.com; p. 14 Petr Jilek/Shutterstock.com; p. 15 rokopix/Shutterstock.com; p. 16 Mariusz Stanosz/Shutterstock.com; p. 17 Lubos Chlubny/Shutterstock.com; p. 18 Dorinda M. Harvey/Shutterstock.com; p. 19 Jed Packer/Shutterstock.com; p. 20 Steve Collender/Shutterstock.com; p. 21 Ghost Bear/Shutterstock.com; p. 22 Sergey Uryadnikov/Shutterstock.com; p. 23 KarSol/Shutterstock.com; p. 24 Jim Barber/Shutterstock.com; p. 25 M. Leonard Photography/Shutterstock.com; p. 26 Steve Boice/Shutterstock.com; p. 29 Bildagentur Zoonar GmbH/Shutterstock.com.

Printed in the United States of America

Some of the images in this book illustrate individuals who are models. The depictions do not imply actual situations or events.

CPSIA compliance information: Batch #CS20GS: For further information contact Gareth Stevens, New York, New York at 1-800-542-2595.

Find us on

CONTENTS

Words in the glossary appear in **bold** type the first time they are used in the text.

SURPRISING FEATS IN THE SKY

As the United States' national bird, bald eagles may seem calm and stately. However, some of their tricks in the sky may surprise you! When trying to find a **mate**, sometimes an eagle will fly high in the air and lock its sharp claws, called talons, with another eagle's. They'll then spin toward the ground together and break away just before hitting the ground!

Read on to learn more unexpected facts about these beautiful birds that are seen as a **symbol** of United States pride and freedom.

4

The practice of eagles locking talons and tumbling, or rolling, together through the air is sometimes called the "cartwheel display" or "death spiral."

NEAT NESTS

FUN FACT: 1

THREE MEN COULD STAND ON EACH OTHER'S SHOULDERS IN THE LARGEST BALD EAGLE NEST EVER FOUND.

The nest, discovered in Florida, was 20 feet (6.1 m) deep and 9.5 feet (2.9 m) in **diameter**. Most nests are up to 4 feet (1.2 m) deep and 6 feet (1.8 m) in diameter.

Bald eagle nests, called aeries, are usually made of sticks, bark, leaves, moss, and grass.

HOW NORTH AMERICAN BIRD NESTS MEASURE UP

BIRD	GENERAL NEST SIZE
BALD EAGLE	5 TO 6 FEET (1.5 TO 1.8 M) ACROSS 2 TO 4 FEET (0.6 TO 1.2 M) DEEP
GOLDEN EAGLE	5 TO 6 FEET (1.5 TO 1.8 M) ACROSS 2 TO 4 FEET (0.6 TO 1.2 M) DEEP
AMERICAN ROBIN	6 TO 8 INCHES (15.2 TO 20.3 CM) ACROSS 3 TO 6 INCHES (7.6 TO 15.2 CM) DEEP
AMERICAN CROW	6 TO 19 INCHES (15.2 TO 48.3 CM) ACROSS 4 TO 15 INCHES (10.2 TO 38.1 CM) DEEP

Bald eagles mate for life. Building the nest is an important way a pair strengthens their bond.

FUN FACT: 2

BALD EAGLE MOTHERS AND FATHERS SHARE THE WORK OF BUILDING THE NEST.

Bald eagle parents usually build their nests near the top of a tall tree by a lake or river, or sometimes on a cliff. They use and build onto the same nest every year.

WHEN THEY HATCH, BALD EAGLE BABIES EACH WEIGH LESS THAN A DECK OF CARDS!

Bald eagle mothers usually lay one to three eggs a year. Newly hatched eaglets are covered with fluffy, light gray feathers called down.

The mother and father take turns **incubating** the eggs for around 35 days. Then the babies, called eaglets, break them open using a tooth they later lose called an egg tooth.

9

THE LIVES OF LIVELY EAGLETS

FUN FACT: 4

WHEN BEING FED, EAGLETS STORE SOME FOOD UNDER THEIR CHINS FOR LATER!

Parents mainly feed their eaglets fish. The eaglets eat as much as they can to grow to be strong. They have a part below the chin, called a crop, where they store extra food to digest, or break down, later.

When an eaglet's crop is full, it looks almost like a golf ball!

Once eaglets start flying, they become fledglings. Fledglings are birds that have flown once but are still under their parents' care.

"BRANCHING" IS THE WAY EAGLETS PRACTICE THEIR FLYING SKILLS!

Branching is when eaglets leave the nest and jump to nearby tree branches flapping, or waving, their wings. This strengthens the wing **muscles** eaglets will one day use to fly!

FUN FACT: 6

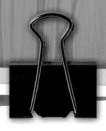

YOUNG EAGLES ARE BORN WITH THE DRIVE TO HUNT AND LEARN BY WATCHING THEIR PARENTS.

It takes 4 to 12 weeks for young eagles to learn how to hunt. Parents will still provide some food to young eagles who are learning.

Adult eagles are skilled hunters and can dive down at around 100 miles (160 km) per hour to catch fish!

12

When a young bald eagle loses feathers to grow a new plumage pattern, it's called molting.

BALD EAGLES DON'T GET THEIR FAMOUS WHITE-FEATHERED HEADS UNTIL THEY'RE AROUND 4 OR 5 YEARS OLD.

Before bald eagles look like the U.S. symbol, their plumage, or the feathers that cover their bodies, is a mixed brown and white pattern that changes several times.

13

WONDERS OF THE WINGS

FUN FACT: 8

A BALD EAGLE'S WINGSPAN NEARLY EQUALS AN AFRICAN ELEPHANT'S HEIGHT!

A bald eagle's wingspan is 6 to 8 feet (1.8 to 2.4 m)! Adult African elephants stand about 8.2 to 13 feet (2.5 to 4 m) tall.

A bald eagle's long, wide wings allow it to save energy while flying high in the sky.

14

A bald eagle's body is 3 to 4 feet (0.9 to 1.2 m) long—around half the length of its wingspan! Female eagles are usually bigger than males.

THE WAY A BALD EAGLE FLIES CAN HELP YOU SPOT IT IN THE SKY!

Eagles are raptors, or birds that kill and eat other animals. Other raptors, such as turkey vultures, fly with their wings slightly raised in a "V" shape, but bald eagles keep their wings flat.

15

EXCELLENT EYESIGHT

IF YOU COULD SEE LIKE AN EAGLE, YOU COULD PROBABLY SPOT A SMALL BUG FROM THE TOP OF A 10-STORY BUILDING!

A bald eagle's eyesight can be up to eight times better than a human's! This lets them spot tasty fish from high in the sky.

Bald eagles have around five times as many nerves in their eyes as people do. Nerves send messages to the brain, so eagles get more facts on what they see.

Other birds also have nictitating membranes. This eyelid helps keep their eyes safe.

BALD EAGLES HAVE THREE EYELIDS!

Bald eagles have an upper and a lower eyelid similar to people, but they also have a special third eyelid called the nictitating membrane. This clear eyelid sweeps across an eagle's eyes and cleans them.

17

DETERMINED DINERS

BALD EAGLES WILL "SWIM" TO PICK UP A HEAVY FISH!

If a bald eagle seizes a fish that's too heavy to lift, sometimes it won't let go. Instead, it will go in the water with the fish and hold on, rowing with its wings to the nearest shore.

Eagles' bones are hollow. This helps them float when in the water with a heavy fish.

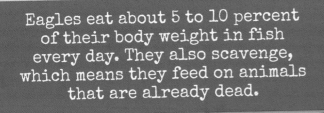

BALD EAGLES HAVE BEEN KNOWN TO STEAL FOOD FROM OTHER RAPTORS.

While they are crafty hunters, bald eagles sometimes chase down other raptors such as ospreys or even other eagles until the other birds drop their food!

TIRELESS TRAVELERS

FUN FACT: 14

WHILE SOME BALD EAGLES DON'T TRAVEL FAR AT ALL, OTHERS FLY MORE THAN 100 MILES (160 KM) A DAY!

Young eagles are known for traveling a lot. Some bald eagles from Florida have been spotted as far north as Michigan! Others have traveled from California to Alaska.

Unlike other birds, bald eagles have less regular migration patterns, or areas where they travel seasonally. They mainly travel to where they're most likely to find food.

Thermals are rising currents of warm air the sun creates when it heats a part of the ground. Riding thermals, eagles can travel at 30 miles (48 km) per hour!

EAGLES NEED WIND IN ORDER TO TRAVEL FAR.

Bald eagles save major travel for clear and sunny days with strong air currents they can ride called thermals. This saves energy and helps them fly high and far!

ADAPTABLE RAPTORS

ALASKA HAS THE LARGEST NUMBER OF BALD EAGLES IN THE UNITED STATES. FLORIDA COMES IN SECOND.

Bald eagles love Alaska because there are a lot of places to live near water without people. Florida is also popular because there are many miles of coastline to hunt fish.

22

Bald eagles have been spotted in all 50 states except Hawaii. They're skilled at adapting, or changing to fit **environments**.

Bald eagle prey, or the animals they hunt and kill for food, varies depending on where the eagles live. Sometimes bald eagles will eat other birds, such as gulls and geese.

BALD EAGLES HAVE SPECIAL BEAKS TO SWALLOW BITES OF THEIR FOOD WHOLE!

Bald eagles don't have teeth to chew their food. Instead, their sharp, curved beaks allow them to poke through the skin of their prey, tearing meat into bite-sized pieces they can swallow whole.

23

THE MAKING OF A NATIONAL BIRD

A BALD EAGLE FIRST APPEARED AS A U.S. SYMBOL IN 1782.

In 1782, Charles Thomson, **secretary** of Congress, had to choose what the nation's seal would look like. A man named William Barton's idea included an eagle to show power. Thomson liked it and used it for the seal.

Thomson made sure the eagle shown on the seal was a bald eagle because it's native to North America. The bald eagle is also an important symbol to Native Americans.

24

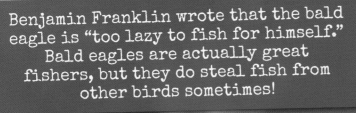

Benjamin Franklin wrote that the bald eagle is "too lazy to fish for himself." Bald eagles are actually great fishers, but they do steal fish from other birds sometimes!

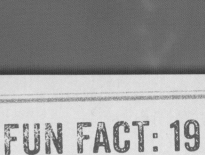

FUN FACT: 19

FOUNDING FATHER BENJAMIN FRANKLIN DIDN'T LIKE THE BALD EAGLE AS THE NATION'S SYMBOL.

In 1784, Franklin wrote in a letter that he thought the bald eagle showed "bad moral character" by stealing from other birds.

TAKING FLIGHT FROM EXTINCTION

IN THE 1960s AND EARLY 1970s, BALD EAGLES FACED EXTINCTION, BUT NOW MANY POPULATIONS ARE GROWING!

Reasons for the decrease included hunting and the use of the pesticide, or bug-killing spray, called DDT. In 1972, the U.S. government banned DDT. Bald eagle populations bounced back!

26

Laws have helped bald eagle numbers rise. In 2007, they were taken off of the **endangered species** list.

HOW DDT AFFECTED BALD EAGLES

FARMERS SPRAYED DDT ON CROPS TO KILL BUGS. → DDT ENTERED WATERWAYS FROM FIELD RUNOFF.

↓

DDT ENTERED FISH ENVIRONMENTS AND THE FISH BALD EAGLES HUNTED.

BALD EAGLES TOOK IN DDT WHEN EATING THE FISH. ←

↓

DDT CAUSED BALD EAGLE EGGS TO HAVE SHELLS THAT WERE TOO THIN. → THE EGGS BROKE EASILY AND THE BALD EAGLE POPULATION WENT DOWN.

↓

BALD EAGLES' EGGS BECAME STRONG AND HEALTHY AGAIN. ← THE U.S. GOVERNMENT BANNED DDT IN 1972.

↓

THE BALD EAGLE POPULATION BEGAN TO GROW!

A CONSERVATION STAR

The bald eagle's comeback is seen as a successful story of conservation, or keeping plants and animals safe.

However, bald eagles still face many human-made dangers. They're sometimes hit by cars or harmed by pollution. People also destroy areas where eagles live to build their own homes or other buildings. Saving bald eagles will take more work in years to come, but the bald eagle's abilities and symbolism certainly keep people driven to fight for them and the natural world they depend on.

You can help keep bald eagles safe by speaking up if you hear that a mall or other building will be built in an area where they live.

GLOSSARY

diameter: the distance from one side of a round object to another through its center

endangered species: a group of animals of the same kind that are in danger of dying out

environment: the natural world in which a plant or animal lives

extinction: the death of all members of a species, or kind, of animal

hatch: to break open or come out of

incubate: to keep eggs warm so they can hatch

mate: one of two animals that come together to produce babies. Also, to come together to make babies.

muscle: one of the parts of the body that allow movement

secretary: a person chosen to be in charge of a particular government department

symbol: a picture, shape, or object that stands for something else

FOR MORE INFORMATION

BOOKS

Amstutz, Lisa J. *A Day in the Life of a Bald Eagle: A 4D Book*. North Mankato, MN: Pebble, 2019.

Cesky, Brittany. *The Bald Eagle*. Minneapolis, MN: Pop!, 2019.

Yasuda, Anita. *Bald Eagle*. Minneapolis, MN: Core Library, 2017.

WEBSITES

Animals for Kids: Bald Eagle
ducksters.com/animals/bald_eagle.php
This site will help you find answers to some common questions you may have about bald eagles.

American Trail: Bald Eagle
nationalzoo.si.edu/animals/bald-eagle
Learn more about these majestic raptors on this site from the Smithsonian's National Zoo.

National Geographic Kids: Bald Eagle
kids.nationalgeographic.com/animals/birds/bald-eagle/
Find out more about bald eagles and check out a map of all the places in North America where they live!

INDEX